THE BODY'S
SYMMETRY

THE BODY'S SYMMETRY

Verandah Porche

HARPER COLOPHON BOOKS
Harper & Row, Publishers
New York, Evanston, San Francisco, London

First HARPER COLOPHON edition published 1974

LIBRARY OF CONGRESS CATALOG CARD NUMBER: 73–17855

STANDARD BOOK NUMBER: 06–090370–8

Designed by Ann Scrimgeour

For J.K.A. and Baby O.

Contents

Part III   PEELING OFF THE LAYERS

Part I
UNDERTOW

UNDERTOW

Brittle-boned, thigh-deep, and
Wading, bird-like, my father stood
While ocean bit and spat the beach about.
The sun bled on his back
Worn pale from years in hiding.

Now bronze and mole-speckled,
He watches the water leering—
Black, unloving mirror,
Unlike Mama's eyes, which tempered
To near sight, no longer see—
Gorgon, unsparing, mocks in a whirlpool,
Eye, shoulder, elbow, torso,
Perseus, my father.

No Circe,
Barebacked seahorse woman,
Mama paddles porpoise-like,
No Aphrodite,
Wet skirt clings to her billowing thighs,
Perhaps a second cousin to the sea,
She muses.

Above, the sun and moon
Divide the sky.
Late afternoon,
The ocean eats her young.

Caught in the throat
Of a gigantic inhalation,
My father topples,
Groping, crippled, for Mama,
Whose arms around him lug him
Trembling, toward the shore.

Ocean pulls the sand against each step.
Salt-blind and tripping,
Mama loosens her grip.
My father floats between her arms,
Surrendering limp and fading
To the seaward thrust.

He didn't drown in the mouth of a wave.
Nine long lifeguards
Answered Mama's shrieks.
Rushing from their canvas chairs,
They linked together
Elbow, shoulder,
And waded
To the place where my father floated
Numb and faceless.
They towed him back.

Safe in a home of bathtubs and seascapes,
Mama mails the postcards
She forgot to send.
Weary from an evening of crosswords
And comedies,
My father climbs the stairs.
Reduced to underwear,
Suntan fading,
He puts himself to bed.

Ear, like a seashell
Pressed to the pillow,
Hears the thrash and babble of a wave.
Blankets sprawl around him
Wrinkled like ripples.
Eyes folded
And falling,
The undertow, swirling about him,
Glides my father into sleep.

BIRTHDAY POEM
FOR MY BIG BROTHER

All grown up and oversized a bit,
No longer naughty
Or delusional,

At twelve you discovered me,
A kitten imp ten years away,
And peddled me, a basketful,
On your bicycle,
Or bathed me in warm water.

On reaching manhood
With yarmulke and tallis,
You bellowed through the Bible,
Lord's avenger.
The rabbi walked you home.
I spilled grape juice on my party dress.
The candles waned
And God was dead.

When fourteen you brewed madness
In the basement,
Like Einstein or Frankenstein:
Long nose, elbows, and disheveled hair.
The bathroom reeked with H_2SO_4.
I was your test-tube babe,
Developed in a darkroom.

At fifteen you gave me up for Marx.
I babbled all the Spanish Civil War tunes
While you leaned on the piano,
Forehead in your right hand.
The revolution thundered from the left.
I volunteered for Eagle Scouts.

The summer of the glorious vacation,
I was six and puking everywhere
From Maine to Mexico.
At Yellowstone I gored my toe.
You painted it with gentian violet,
And made my mouth prune-purple
Like a fallen lady-woman's lips.

I did not understand the day
They packed your bags,
And you, big brother,
Skinny in your double-breasted suit,
Kissed my face.
I swore fidelity and vowed to wait,
As you saddled the black Oldsmobile,
Excalibur, a slide rule at the hip,
And galloped toward the plains
Of Academia,

Never to return
As Father,
Oracle,
Magician,
Hero,
Healer,
Or Husband.

Brother, we are grown,
And barking up the right trees.

You tame numbers.
I make poems.

SUNDAY MORNING:
EARLY WAKING

Lingering abed with memory,
Quilted in the warmth of Sunday waking,
I see your house diminished to a doll's,
The back wall cut away,
Furniture movable with a pinky.

Tiny in her nightgown,
Mama draws a robe about her
To collect the *Times* outdoors
And scramble eggs.
Dusting in the living room,
She pauses
Before photographs of parents and progeny.
Mama wipes our glossy faces
As if we all had runny noses,
Or if by rubbing, she could call us there.
She sets us on the piano back.
With grand arpeggios she sweeps the keys,
Unable to resist a Chopin waltz.
When doll-sized, I curled beneath the piano
While the room vibrated in a polonaise.
Now it stands like a shiny dying animal.
She cleans the teardrops off the chandelier.

My father stays in bed an extra hour,
The lordly *Times* propped up against his knees
That once were a fortress for small children.
He wanders through the magazine,
Filling half the crossword blanks in ink.
From a long shower and ample brunch,
He follows to the piano
For "Melancholy Baby" in the key of F,
Or "All I Want's a Paper Doll."
The lyrics shake the chandelier.

Over your shoulder by piano and sink,
I stand by you this morning,
A paper doll grown to a giantess,
Now shrunk to child-size
By the dream of Sunday waking.

ABOUT SOME MISCHIEF

For Phoebe Snow

Skirts hitched up
And ankles showing many petticoats,
We princesses
Scampered up the shoulder
Of a sleeping hill,
Flopped down like rag dolls,
Scurried through the orchard,
And hid like skinnies
Disguised as peach trees.

Phoebe, what a funny dance.

One last glance
At the smoke-stacked chimney
And we darted off like orphans
On cats' paws
Into the forest green,
Green and foreboding
As the gates of Oz.

A maple, stern and owl-wise
As brother Martin,
Caught your heel in his hand.

"A penny for my thoughts,"
He said.
"A stitch in time is worth a dime.
A picture is a grain of salt.
A bird in the brain
Is worth two in the bush.
No rest for the weary.
All roads lead from home."

Mama waxed the forest floor.
We slipped with roller-skating speed.
A little bird perched on a stone sang,
"You left your galoshes home."
Mama chased us in between the birches
With a rolling pin.

A fearsome wind
Like Father's blast-into-a-hanky sneeze,
Rattled the windows of the woods
Blowing our skirts above our knees.

"Mon Dieu!" cried Phoebe.
"Let us get us home!"

Two little Gretels
Without a bag of bread crumbs,
We sat on a log with our thinking caps
While the sun broke its yolk
On the treetops.

O dank woods,
There is mischief in your timbers
And surprise.
The moon lights the pupils
Of meat-hunting animal eyes.

A rustle in the underbrush.
Our sad hearts beat like cuckoo clocks,
And then a hush.

Of all creatures kind as a dolphin,
From nowhere there appeared a doe
Lithe and surefooted as sister Alice,
Whose ears bade us follow her nose
From the cranky woods.

Bound for the quilts and pantries of home,
The pleases and may I's,
The liver and spinach,
Ran two world-weary princesses.
Phoebe gave the doe a candy kiss.

The stars stood out like dotted Swiss
On the hilltop.
Frost crackled the peach boughs.
Phoebe cried,
"A hop, skip, and jump
Away from home,
The world is wild."

LOVE SONG FOR
AUTUMN AND WILLIAM

Climbing down by branch and root the hill,
William led me to a river ringed by cattails
That we trampled as we sat,
And willows drooping over us
Like hair.
William pulled the pins
That held my hair,
And turned my face
To his.

He was a prince of autumn dressed in leaves.
A gesture of his hand made summer
Blush and seasons change.
The willows bent to touch his knees.
They hid us from the park police
As we rolled wrapped in his overcoat,
Kissing until the stars fell out,
When it got too cold
To kiss.

William combed the willows from my hair,
Replaced the pins,
And drew a smile across my face
For mother,
Dropped a curtsy to my lord,
Then one more kiss atop the hill
For autumn and William,
Who was gone by frost.
William, William, who was gone by frost.

A GENTLE ODE

An age before the arms of fine young men,
You rescued me from pointed knees,
Our father's unresilient lap,
To dangle me,
Your secret pet,
Or scratch the surface
Of my unsuspecting flesh.

Brother, how you loved me then.
Our sins are trivial,
Yet unforgiven.

I lie tonight
In the arms of a man
Who plays my body
Like a mandolin.

I was small comfort to your bachelorhood.
Our evening games of peek-a-boo
And tickle me.
I would have stayed,
You sent me off for good.

And off again to play
Beneath the sea,
Consort with cod
Or caviar.

There is a pain
Like a baited hook
Stuck in the side,
Where the skin's grown hard
And tight.
It only hurts
On very rainy nights.

A RHYME FOR BABY JONATHAN

I walk the street both up and down,
Beneath my feet the cobbles sound,
But I will never get to town
For I can't cross the street.

On the curb I am a king,
My head is high, a song I sing,
For on the road there's not a thing
To make me run away.

Mommy says that when I'm ten
She'll let me cross the street and then
I'll march with all the tallest men,
Triumphant into town.

DIDO'S END

Soft in the counterpanes of memory
He sleeps. The hero lingers in my lair.
I reach to trace his jaw, but grasp the air
With empty-handed fists, heart's travesty.

For you, Aeneas, I have left my veil
And widow's vow, to wait among the deeds
You scattered at my feet like fertile seeds:
Just now, as they take root, your ships set sail.

Spin, Sister Fates, complete the treachery
Of in-laws, arms, and warriors. Sley the loom.
Weave a garment worthy of my name
To fit him, wear him, shroud him on the sea.

Anna, bring that rubbish here to burn.
May he see my fire and return.

Part II
NOBLE SAVAGES

NOBLE SAVAGES

"You know you is
The only baby I love . . ."

I. HER LESSON

Each evening as the sun reclined,
A ripe tomato on a limp vine,
She met him with a bag of words
By the patched screen door
And the struggling rose.
His eyes gleamed with crosses.
Ernesto,
Red-handed as Esau.

She plotted his course on the table top
From the poor house farm
To the promised land,
As he was keen-witted and handsome.

Her lesson: to have, to need, to want.
She balanced her heart like a teacup.
Ernesto,
Bull in a china shop.

Puerto Rico is my home,
America, my Uncle Sam.
Pellegrino is my boss.
His daughter rides a golden horse.

23

Rice and beans,
Beans and rice,
Cervéza with a Lucky Strike,
Washington Street on a Saturday night,
Mi vida.

To have, to need, to want.

I have a good heart.
I need a woman.
I want a wife.
Querida maestra.

II. HER CONFESSION

Ernesto, though I seemed prim,
My lover was prim and fancy.
As he sailed his boat by lilypads,
I read Vozneshensky.
His mother scorned me for his lust.

In wavering grass
I gave up the ghost
At the tomb of the freedman slave.

A wallful of uncles
Accost me.

How well I remember our last supper.
My hand lay in yours,
A little glass slipper.
Your hand was big as a boxing glove.

I smoothed my skirts around me
Like a fan
And fastened my eyes to the future,
Querida maestra.

WINTER SUITE

I.

How changeless as a broken clock
These houses stand—
The hour infested alleyways
Of laundromat and liquor store.
A pigeon alights on the fire escape.
The room is drafty
As the halls of winter.

The weather froze last week.
We woke to hieroglyphics on the windows,
Intricate and formal
As a map of the tenfold fall of Troy,
Banished so swiftly
At the warmth of his hand.

II.

Where are we going?

He does not answer,
Only the radio bantering ads.
Parallel on the telephone poles,
Wires shoot voices,
Lip to ear.

The scenes we pass so swiftly
Are postcards from the wilderness—
"Dry fields weary of harvest,"
"A young man strolling, lonely
By the edge of an echoing lake,"

Then the trees, redundant
And so painfully alive,
They seem my sisters.

Leaves like golden coins,
I leave my watermark among them.

Older than ancient,
The forest floor
Must be lined with the bones
Of mastodons,
And in their wake
These trees sprang up,
Haunted ones,
Their branches laced together
In the sun.

III.

While sharing a spot of tea
By the sea,
I made this rhyme:

Ocean, seasoned with ice and salt,
Is there no place left to go?
My feet are frozen to the knee
And seaweed sticks between my toes.

When Virginia Woolf entered the Ouse
She shed her hat and parasol.
If ever I enter your opening arms,
I will give you all.

IV.

All the ride over to Boston
I slept on his lap,
Then woke seeing red
As a stoplight shot
Through the windshield.

White buildings
Immaculate as an empty automat.

It started to sleet.
I caught a cold.

If there is any season,
I would call it winter.

THE EAGLE SCOUT IN SEASON

He knew the secret vows,
The handshake,
The salute.

Broad-winged was my Eagle Scout,
The midnight bird
Who made my bed
His roost.

He had an eye for nature,
Keen to twisted roots and undersides
Of leaves,
And glad was he,
As every mother's son,
About the mysteries of two
Becoming one
Or three.

Who learned the promises by heart:
To help young ladies walk the streets,
To tie the hair in granny knots.
His pledge-allegiance lips
Made merit badges on my sleeves.
To brush his teeth
Before he went to bed.

When he rose to the task,
That faithful bugler,
Between his taps and reveilles,
He wrapped my body in old glory
As if I were some unknown soldier:
Only he could lift me from the dead.

Beyond steep palisades of sleep,
We chased the wild beast of Bear Mountain,
Where hand to horn to mouth
In the high wind
He blew tattoo,
And shaking his feathered head,
He flew the way of all birds
Out of season.

POEM IN THE MORNING

Lying in your arms
This morning,
I am happier than usual.
From all the groceries of sleep
You call me:
Pomona, Persimmon, Papaya, Nectarine.
The breasts are citric,
Belly, melon-like,
My eyes, my hands
Are ripe.
Dozing in your arms
That gather me,
I think how strange it is
We do not love.

PARK STREET UNDER

Because no love is left
To make,
We take to trains.

No weather in the underground,
But chill-damp blasts of pizza
From the Rainbow Bar
Waft down the stairways
Where we catch our trains.

Bowed by woolens and galoshes,
Your hands and feet forget
How, joined by the hip
At homecoming,
We wanted
No exit.

The doors slide shut
As guillotines
Severing from sight
Your face.
Our paths twist and wander
Under the city.

If you love me
In the summer,
Take the nightmare turn
At Boylston Street.
Meet me at Park Street Under
Where the third rail lives.

DOUBLE EXPOSURE

Blue as the stars
Of late movies,
These faces blink and reel
From remembrance:

A car door slams in the driveway.
He rents a latch key to the inn.
A bellhop grins.
She follows him.
Evening falls like linen
On the bed.

An eternal submission
Of buttons, laces, hooks, and eyes,
The garments tossed aside
Are flotsam.

A cage of ribs
Is a flimsy jail,
Said warden to maiden.
She peers through the rungs.
He turns a key
To set her free.

The bedsprings yawn
Like hinges.

*   *   *   *

These characters, once bold,
Revolve beneath the film
Of waking lids:

Translucent figures rise
From a divided bed,
Turn and tighten the blankets
To hide a melodrama on the sheets.
Hands scrub faces,
Shave,
Or bind the hair with pins,
Stuff bedclothes in valises.

Four eyes explore the room,
Again anonymous—
A chambermaid with a mop and pail,
A key ring on the window sill,
They snap them shut.

A shuddering sight,
The double exposure of midnight
And morning.
The lovers,
Spliced and severed,
Return and revolt.

IN ABSENTIA

I.

It's not for love
Of you,
But for the lack
Of arms and ankles
After sleep,
That I recall the corners
Of your smile turned down
Like blankets
On a waiting bed.

II.

When I remember
How you tasted—
Of winter and supper,
Toothpaste and salt—
It is difficult to breathe.

OVER PLATO'S SYMPOSIUM

For Richard Wizansky

I'm brushing my teeth
For Plato dozing
Draped in a toga
Of sheets and quilts.
Soon I'll plait my hair,
Tonight to court him,
Purified by rites, anointments,
Dinner and a brief appointment.

If only I could share your time,
Shelve my lover,
My rituals of grief,
My suicide,
To join you for an hour.

Bring to me my other half,
My twin,
My beast,
My back.

Take me to the party
I missed that year at Agathon's,
You oracle,
Plato,
My Greek.

ALTAMIRA

Altamira
in your eyes, love,
you are the hunter.
I see in your wanting,
hands holding fire.
The cave-in-heart
gives chase to the buffalo
fleeing my hunger
across the wall.

ON AN ELECTRIC BLANKET

Complacent friend,
you do not snore
or stir from sleep
like my young man.
Warm me
with your stripes of heat,
Or flee in the chill
of dawn
With a red-faced fare-thee-well.
Pink
and softer than his flesh,
Electrify my chastity.

THE TRANSPLANTED HEART

In which a lady
Relates her past
To the handsome stranger
Over pots and pans

I.

The cat gave birth before me.
It was dead, her kitty,
So tiny, encapsulated, and undone.

She dragged it to a corner
Where she ate it with gusto.
Much better than Calo.
She made it herself.

II.

One winter night
Without farewell,
I tossed my psyche in a satchel—
A hairbrush,
A hundred bucks,
A good dress,
And ploughed my way
Through the six states of confusion
That split the map
From Boston to D.C.

III.

We made a baby once
Who lived for years inside us,
Tiny flower.
He called her Imogene
Who died so full of good advice.
She would have loved him as I did
So I had the operation,
And blew through the park
Like a leaf.

IV.

We weren't always cigarettes
And broken hearts.
I remember the nights
He washed my hair
And combed the knot
Before it dried.

It was nice while it lasted.
She would have been a looker.
No, you're right, we were crazy.

Now the carrots are burning.
We're late for supper.
Come, carry a pitcher of tears.

TO R. WITH PEN AND PAPER

I have lain long with Thucydides
Rehearsing ancient wars,
Now wander, book and window
To your face,
Bent brow in fist.

Snow drops in slow motion
Sleeving roof and ledges.
Clothes freeze at attention
On the lines.

Thucydides mocks poets
For loose-witted histories
As you fix your brainwaves
Into verse.

Weary of the catapults and battlements
I yawn.
Soon you notice
There has been a storm.

A SOFT SHOE

For Morris,
Prince of the Ward

"If no man is an island,"
Cried Morris Irving Hyman,
"I'm the narrowest peninsula
In the world."

Oh they've put you away again,
Morris, minus mind,
Another year in the corridors
Where ends don't meet.

All the nurses know you're smart.
They let you keep your mattress
On the floor
Where germs are.

Last night you kissed
The lisping blonde
Who penned her letter to the world
In blood.
Tomorrow you will love her,
Lend her comic books,
And next week,
Lay her
In the elevator.

Morris,
Will you dance together
Giggling off the roof,
To prove
How well you know
The world is flat?

GRAY MATTER

Death is sinking
In a feather bed

I cannot tell you
Why the doors grew blades
Each time I entered,
Or why the chair attacked me
With its arms.

These gray-green walls
Sting with the scent of hospital,
Cripples stitched together
Wave their hook hands
As I climb the stairs
And settle in the rocking chair
Which creaks.

The eaves of my room
Are still as a cathedral.
Tonight before sleep,
Michelangelo
Sketches his face
On a shirt of skin.

WINDOW POEM
FROM THOMAS CIRCLE

Washington, D.C., 1968

Green with age
And frozen in the saddle,
With a humble nod
For a hundred-gun salute,
Long silent,
Sits the model major general
Hat in hand.

There is little to praise, sir,
Washington's needle,
The Santa María,
The President,
The mint,
The tombs.

If we do not smite
The gorgon of cities,
Gray-feathered eagles
Will carry us off
To make glue and soap
Of our sleep.

I am a simple woman
Not given to murder, martyrdom,
Or apocalyptic dreams,
Yet in well-lit rooms
At midday,
The images ooze like auto fumes
As they circle the green,

Where General Thomas
Watches the traffic
Awaiting the moment
To dive through the dome
Of the Hotel America pool.

A PATRIOTIC ODE

To Ray Mungo

When in the Course of Human Events,
It's a good day, Ray.
Though cars collide
Like warring dinosaurs,
The Fourth of July
On the Lower East Side
Must be grand.

So far, so long in the wilderness,
I hide in my traitor's bed
From the boom,
For the fireworks have belched
An avalanche of eagles
To swoop me away from my dreams
Of your chinny chin chin
And your old soft shoe.

Spell it again—
It's a good day, Ray,
Where the eagles bit
My sides are torn
Like ruffles from a petticoat.
Only your Jack-be-nimble
Stitch in time
Can fasten back my glory
To the flag.

Carry me back from the wilderness
And into your lair,
For every boy scout needs a brownie,
Sadder but wiser,
I'm still your girl.

Fiddle me back
With your half-cocked hat,
Then after a pause for a candy bar,
We'll pay the piper for the feast
And shuffle off
From Buffalo to Mars.

ELEGY FOR A SEMI-SUICIDE

Today the papers featured on page 1,
Your photo,
Pompadour and grin.
Your face has aged.
The smile sags at the corners.

Arthur,
Anointed with gasoline,
You chose a poet's death.

Before the flame could sear
The crabgrass off the White House lawn,
As Johnson resurrected Christ in Texas,
They rescued you.

At rest in Saint Elizabeth's,
Did you recall the bloodlettings,
Or tears that left the matchbook
Without light?

No matter, Arthur,
Two-fisted orators divide the earth.
One hand offers chocolate,
The other, death.
Both hands will not grasp
The verdict:
Mad, if patriotic.

POEM IN DESPAIR

Jets again—
We nail the windows shut,
Plug knuckles in our ears,
And still
The chilled drone
Rattles through our dreams.

They knew the angel once
In Egypt.
They smeared the doors with blood.
They hid, or begged,
Pass over us.

Somewhere in a village
Remote as the mountains of the moon,
The grim migration
Ends in eggs.

Again,
The phantoms over Boston.

TO R. WHEN FEET
ARE ROLLER SKATES

Leave swiftly,
Neither weatherproof
Nor comforted

Tonight we have a slender feast
Of breakfast food,
Hardly a home-cooked meal.
I cannot offer you a change of sheets
Or a wench to warm
And wrinkle them with you.

I notice the valise parked by the bed
With a label
That says pack and flee.

Shall I hold the baby in one arm
And shake the other fist
As you pass on?

There is no child.
There never was one.

You nourish me.
Your madness makes the blood
Run rings around my heart:
I will not cease
Your circulation.

METAMORPHOSES

I.   THE BLACK SHEEP

If I am not your little lamb,
It is not that I do not choose to be.
I would ease the vigil
Of your shepherd's nights,
Frolicking in gentle sodomy,
Dance to your flute,
Or tend the fires that tame
The mountain top.

When you turn your eyes
To court the moon or long for home,
I feel the fangs.
As Jekyll bristled into Hyde,
My fleecing stiffens to a pelt.

And in the morning,
Beg forgiveness
For the sins that passed unnoticed—
Lamb and canine.

II. THE BAD NYMPH

As Daphne darted through the forest
Crying, Pater,
Save me from this fate,
You thought she wanted her virginity
Enshrined in laurel,
Fool.

Afraid Apollo might give up the chase,
She chose a form he couldn't forget.
Those gods were always searching
For new sport.
How novel then to be a tree.

Her bark was better than his bite.
She won the race.

My arms are branches.
Can you see my face?

III. THE WHITE ROCK SIREN

Though I have known little
Of ocean and death,
If you wrap my throat with seaweed,
I will sing you rocks and shipwrecks,

"The long lost hymns
On the waterlogged lips
Of a suicide . . ."

It is for poets
To mix ocean with soda,
Make death from dream,
Then love from the alchemy of both,
And never share the recipe.

MADRIGAL

Farewell to the Jeweler's Son,
I leave you in a rage,
These humble, handpicked lines of verse
I spat across the page.

> Come kiss me anyway,
> Come kiss me anyway,
> Cartier, Cartier, Cartier

Gentle-spoken Jeweler's Son,
Tonight the room is lit
With memory of your flowing mouth,
Your bow and arrow wit.

> Come kiss me anyway,
> Come kiss me anyway,
> Cartier, Cartier, Cartier

Glancing once into your eyes
When we were quite alone,
I noticed they reflected light
Like overpolished stone.

> Come kiss me anyway,
> Come kiss me anyway,
> Cartier, Cartier, Cartier

Last night you rolled me in your arms,
Today you play the lord,
Exploring cultural affairs
With Helena of Ford.

                              Come kiss me anyway,
                              Come kiss me anyway,
                              Cartier, Cartier, Cartier

Your life is like a two-way street,
No roadblocks interfere—
At nightfall the conquistador,
At dawn the cavalier.

                              Come kiss me anyway,
                              Come kiss me anyway,
                              Cartier, Cartier, Cartier

Gallop toward the sweaty sun
Astride your clubfoot steed,
And seek to suit your fantasy
A lady more in need.

                              Come kiss me anyway,
                              Come kiss me anyway,
                              Cartier, Cartier, Cartier

'Twould be bad form, my Careful One,
To end a verse so mean.
I send it with my compliments:
Your nails were always clean.

> Come kiss me anyway,
> Come kiss me anyway,
> Cartier, Cartier, Cartier

Part III

PEELING OFF
THE LAYERS

INVOCATION

Night fits down
Like a tight lid
Over our valley, cauldron-deep.
We gather kindling sticks
To earn our sleep.

God help us
Refugees in winter dress
Skating home on thin ice
From the Apocalypse.

FOR THE FIRST OF AUTUMN

The still hand takes a lesson bitterly—
Six months silent,
Dormant, stranded as in a root cellar,
Like the monster squash
We cannot slice,
Useless as the wobbling hens
We'll kill tomorrow
Every day.

(My fingers find themselves suddenly
Prehensile.)

A spider scales the window sill
Feeling for the place
Her web was,
Where she tied the speckled moth
In knots,
Who ate the elbow from my favorite dress.
Homeless.
I wiped her network from the corner
With an old sock yesterday.
She patiently surveys
The wreckage.

Lady, if you will spin a parlor,
Soon the gyspy moth
Will climb your ladder,
Climb to court you
In an idle hour,
Listen to your sorrows,
Be your dinner.

Lady, embroider my window
With your lethal stitch.
Let it be a sign
For those who doubt us.

I will keep your secrets.

FIRST FIRE

Spring passed through
Like a traveling salesman,
Woodstove damped and empty
As an ashcan.
Summer, torrid as roof tar,
Sealed the mouth.
Skin wore like a wet suit.

Black frost finally seized
The tomatoes,
Sunset, easy over,
Moonlight spills into evening
Like milk in cider jugs
To chill.

The tin stove glows inside
With images of Armageddon.
Fresh split logs
Crackle like bacon,
Kindled by hymns,
And prothalamions undone.

LA BELLE CHINOISE

For Ellen Snyder

Ah, for the weaver of hyperbole,
How difficult to seek the metered song
To celebrate that Chinese lady.

Wild geese flew over our mountain.
We dropped our hoes and gaped.
Enfevered petals floated from the trees. . .

I have no words.
How chilling beauty passes
From our days.

Lady, from untutored lips,
Silence is the only praise.

WINDOW POEM

For Pete Gould
over "Burnt Toast"

Where wind has rasped
Consumptive o'er the fields
For weeks,
Now utter calm is in the corn stalks.
The still life of an afternoon,
Evening impending.

Thorn reeds frozen stiff
As hair in fright
Rise from the pate
Of Father Time.

Unfathomable ice in the spring box,
Wherein a frog,
Gone hard as rubber,
Dreams of sun
Rippling on his speckled back,
Or of inland algae.

Here fire rumbles in the stove
Like hunger,
The high-built bed
Longs for a lover.
Here, with ikons watching,
Young Silent prints his words
On onionskin,
Where I
From pen and rocking chair
Must fly like woodsmoke,
Fleeing
From the oven of sighs.

CHRISTMAS NIGHT AND
NEW YEAR'S MORNING

Harbinger of the wind,
Carry my poem,
A paper bird
On a Christmas bough,
To flutter in the cage of ribs,
The muscled walls,
And sing.

*   *   *

I waken from his chest
Of bones
As skinny as a xylophone,
To find a minor chord of love
Between the fixed ribs
And the heart.

CHRISTMAS, 1968

Oh, say the imp has come again.
Forgive a truant at the manger.

I gazed at the stars
As the Magi passed.
What interest has a Jewess
In a little *goy?*
Behold, Orion stalks the mountain
Hunting blind.

For centuries I did not celebrate.
Now mellowing the atheistic ice,
As I would seize the drumstick
In my hand and sing,
I have come late,
And bear no offering.

VALENTINE

Oh that the snow
Might flurry down
Like dandruff
On a spinster gown,
Or dust on a dish,
My powdered wig.

I grow old with shawls
And birches nurse me.
Earth,
Innocent as a tabula rasa,
Cannot be blamed.

Kind Harry,
Carry me once more
Over the glass mountain,
Where I will gather,
For your pleasure,
Peaches in winter.

If you will only keep me,
Tiny in the hand as marzipan,
I shall gather,
At my leisure,
Peaches in winter.

FROM THE FEVER BED

To ail and sleep,
It is a lifetime calling

Weary, limp, and wheezing
In the fever bed,
How well I am as an invalid,
With all my Latin viruses,
Old handkerchiefs,
And cold beef tea,
The syrup green
As emerald blood
To comfort me and croon
As I sip sip sip from my silver spoon.

Ah, sweet malaise,
When I sneeze
There are crimson meteors,
Or comets, medicine green.

Lady of anemia,
That child of chicken pox
Has grown,
Now mistress of the blight
No bloodletter can cure
With ointments, leeches, herbs.

Treat it like the flu,
He said,
A week on your back with a book.
When you've had your fill,
It will wear off, wear off
Like a toy tattoo.

After all these years,
My love,
I am finally consumptive.

THE CRADLE SNATCHERS

When the dead are risen
And the living, dead,
Spirits rock my cradle underground.

What hospital is this,
Madonna, murderess?
A troll for a midwife,
Beasts in a manger,
Father, remote as the Holy Ghost,
Conspire to kill my innocents.

A blue flame rises
From the instruments.

Now tamed, and fastened to the stirrups
Of a dead horse mated with nightmare,
I am clamped and scalpeled,
Scissored, washed,
And whisked to the streets
To stand, dumbfound, alone.

My foundling, foundling,
Tiny bastards,
Scooped like cysts from spiteful flesh,
Tots without breath or gender,
Flushed away like the monthly death,
Forgive me,
And be gone.

LULLABY

Gather close
The images that cleave,
The unborn toes and fingers
Of my dreams,
The knees and elbows,
Moonface of an embryo
Somersaulting in the sea,

Soft skeletons, awake,
Remember me.

The dead are risen
And the living, dead.
Spirits rock my cradle underground.

LETTER FROM A FOREIGN CITY

Gentle in the lap of love,
The bed, board and body
Of a man more to my liking—
From the quilts of morning,
I am writing for some fatherly advice.

I have redeemed my days,
Have peeled your life from mine
Like a tangerine,
And go about the kitchen,
Free and graceful as a newlywed
Seasoning the eggs,
Or a virgin,
Seasoning eggs for the first time.

And still,
My nights are twisted
With the image of you riding
Swift as a thief,
Riding west
With my sanity captured in a great sack,
My heart kicking and pounding
Like a ravished waif.

With the image of your fingers
Fastened to my body,
Ten electrodes,
Plotting the score of my womanhood
On a lie detector.

Or the evening truce
Between venom and boredom,
When we curled together
Innocent and happy
As a pair of socks
Fresh from the washer,
The chambers of our hearts,
Adjoining rooms,
A suite
Or minuet,

The nights you loved me
Ruffled in my sleep,
Have left their mark.
I say you ruined me.

I spin my days
On an empty spool,
As a careful seamstress
Ripping a hem
Rewinds the thread
To sew again,

The thread,
So fragile, scarce and dear—
To love is crazy.

Say why,
When you cradle her
To sleep,
It looks so easy.

A BLIZZARD IN THE PAPERWEIGHT

Of the body's symmetry,
I despair,
How arms and legs are strangers
To their mates,
As elbow, ankle, eyelid, ear,
Their twins.

Mirror, I am half a woman
Fastened to an alien.
What interloper
Shares my skin?

These proud, anarchic hands
Have long grown weary of each other
As lover to lover.
Mutineers, they will not knit
Or knead a loaf.
One waits for death,
The other for the dance,
My brittle twigs.

Spare me in my cowardice.
The earth seems girded for an avalanche.
Wind, with the bark
Of feral children,
Shakes apparitions on the snowfields,
Yet restlessness
Would bid me wander out.

So frail a house,
My heart goes strict with fear
That I might open
Like an earthen crock
And fling the stale bread
Of my brain
At the shuddering birds
Grown mute with hunger.

AN ARIA FOR WINTER AND
THE LADY FROM OKLAHOMA

I.

Wind caught in nets

When the heavens opened
Like an Easter egg,

Wind piped through lungs
Of the woods
Like tuberculosis

And the sun fell out
With its yolk
Of broken promises,

Birds huddled in their wings
Like overcoats

A lady came by Greyhound
From Oklahoma

Wind snapping the arms
From the orchard

With a bird brain like a hom-
  ing pigeon,
Looking for her man,
And had we seen him?

Earth hidden in its snow skin
Like a baked potato

Oh, that Bull-in-a-china-
Shop-worn-
Take-your-chance man
Juggled her heart,

Wild cat frozen
Eating a robin,
Ice with teeth

And fiddled his way
Toward Mexico
Where

Lock jaws of the wind

They clapped the scofflaw
Into a bandit's cell

Gatekeeper of the wind	For crimes unrelated to
	season,
	Or the lady
	Who is shaking in her boots
	By the stove
Who is our master	Who will not take bread and
	soup
	At our table
Shelter the lady	Who babbles her story
	Like a schoolgirl
	With a gold star:

II.

Black peach clinging	I have come
To the snow tree	And I have gone
Like a fetus	From Oklahoma
Deer will not eat it	Where my father
Though they are taut	Is king of the rodeo,
With hunger	Where I was his gypsy
Wander on tiptoe	Cowgirl majorette.

Wind bellowing through the
*   pasture*
Like a superhighway

I have traveled the map o'
    mundi,
Oceans, islands, highways
Like snakes or arteries,

Snow seeds glinting
In the evening sun
Like dust

And in the whole world,
There is one face
On one man

Lock jaws of the wind
At nightfall

Who split my heart like a
    walnut
With his squirrel teeth,

Wind trapped in a cage
Of stars

Who nibbled the tenderest
    part
Until it was gone

Wind caught in nets

I wear the shell like a locket,
Sang the lady
From Oklahoma.

TRANSFUSIONS FROM AN HOURGLASS

An elegy for Marshall Bloom

I.

> *"Fix the tractor,*
> *Plow the fields,*
> *And die. . . ."*

Farmer of the mind,
You were,
Hunched down at dawn
Correcting rows and rows
Of cucumbers.

> *"A guy at the mill*
> *Says cukes are good*
> *As cash. . . ."*

For all the sins
Of last year's politics,
You warred with ragweed,
Worried over witchgrass.
Man walked on the moon.

Freak rains of the summer
Drowned our crops,
Yet up sprang cukes,
Not dollar-green,
But yellow submarines.

You hauled them
To the pickle vats
And lined the sacks
With stones.

> *"By hook or by crook,*
> *Or by bread alone,*
> *We must survive. . . ."*

II.

All Souls' Day,
Hunters, eager for deer scent,
Found you resting after breakfast
In the green of your Triumph,
Crumpling the news of massacres.

A vacuum cleaner hose
Hooked tailpipe to wing window,
Gone.

The dogs must have howled blue murder,
But they lied.

What is the scent
Of suicide?

III.

Ten days rain
After your passing,
We rode in cars like lifeboats
Over mud,
Crying,
Settle back into the mire
Of me.

My eyes make silhouettes at noon—
The jack o' lantern sun,
The roots we sowed and dug for food—
Have no relief.

The edge of everything
Is pain:
The imprint molars make
On something soft.

IV.

A wind unráveled autumn
Like a woolen shawl.
Cold shoulders of the hills
Are spare,
The trees as stark
As knives and forks.

A second fall
Has left us humble,
Almost mute,
And single in our beds
As spoons.

Crumpling the news of massacres
Into a ball,
I kneel with tinder
Bellowing to summon fire.
The hiss of damp wood
Dries and wets my eyes.

"Love, if the dead lie close
In their tight ships,
Come now,
Marshall, free in your kayak
Sealed like a peapod,
Know I am landlocked. . . ."

v.

Gone so soon from these mammalian hills.
They slit Caesarean
The belly of an eagle,
Slid you in like a fetus.

The jet hit Denver
Where you honored your parents
With a last appearance—
Gaunt yet muscular
With proud electric hair,
Eschatologic eyes.

All the dead are relatives.
The world is bottom-heavy
From their weight.

They tucked you in with prayers
As parents will,
Beneath the biceps of the Rockies,
One mile high
And six feet under the weather.

vi.

Thunder in the attic
Is an invalid.
No grace is said.
No dinner finishes
Without your image wheeling
In the room.

Frail uncle, maiden aunt,
Memento mori,

You ate our hearts out
For a trifle,
Willed us,
Saprophytes.

VII.

A bedouin
Before a feast he lies,
His smile thin
As the new moon.

I fall to him
Like a comet.

Scarlet,
He names me Scarlet.

PEELING OFF THE LAYERS

I.

Waffled-white,
and intimate as underwear,
we wore the winter
like a pelt,
until the thick of it
became our skins,
the touch of it
had nerves enough.

Huddled at the stove
all still as a circle of gargoyles,
muffled to the fingertips
in counterpane—our coat of arms—
the nails remained
exposed like claws
to turn a page,
or itch among the inches
of our clothes.

What is warm?
The firelight barely reignites a memory.
The menfolk snore like polar bears.
The women dream like schoolmarms.

II.

When your love had turned to water
(cold to hold, yet tangible
as a fistful of ice, it was),
spilled through the broken cup
of palms,

I turned aside my finery,
rolled down remembering
as ladies in a world at war
remove silk stockings,
thin as membrane,
precious as the notion
of love-not-rent
from thigh to toe.

Reclining in the bath,
where gravity is less than earth,
a lady, soap-fleeced,
shorn of stockings,
might admire,
as if it were a mannequin's,
the end
of what was once
a well-turned ankle.

III.

The sun one morning
Ignites a furnace in the east.
We sever us from sleep
and one by one assemble
in the yard
for peeling off the layers
of wool and gloom to flesh.
Our shy bones crack like knuckles
in the heat.
Our muscles twitch like frogs' eyes.

The soil revealed beneath the flood
(snow, gray and weary
as a union suit in May)
is bristled, stubbled, soft
and clammy with matted grass,
as winter legs,
our walking sticks.

MIRAGES

For Raymond A. Mungo

I.

Even sinners walk on water.
Over hills like hard-boiled eggs,
Oases frozen,
Hollows scrubbed and polished
As a tub,
I have trod,
Innocent of pain
As a parsee.

Ice will be the edge of me,
Still in my tracks
As a pillar of salt
For the deer to lick.

II.

Winter held him mummified.
He shed his clothes like bandages
And hooked them to a tree.

Sun, will you wear me?
I would swap skins with the terrapin
Or toad.
The water, still as gelatin,
And cold, commands

We vanish into images,
Oases, amphibians,
Mirages.

74 75 76 77 78 79 80   12 11 10 9 8 7 6 5 4 3 2 1